Primitive people

Primitive people are people who live close to Nature. They know a lot about Nature, about plants and animals.

They live in simple huts. They feed themselves by hunting, fishing, rearing animals or by gathering plants that can be eaten. Some live by simple farming. They make their own tools.

Primitive people's religion had a lot to do with getting a good harvest and avoiding illness and accidents.

Many people in Africa are primitive people. The Indians in North and South America were once primitive people. The Lapps in northern Scandinavia and the Eskimos in Greenland also used to live a primitive life.

The Masai

My name's Samba and I belong to the Masai tribe.
We Masai live in north-eastern Tanzania in Africa.

We're nomads.
That means we raise cattle and that we move them from one grazing ground to another. We raise cows, sheep, goats and donkeys.

We live all together in a tribe or "large family".

The tribe is what makes us secure.
There are lots of rules that we have to follow.
If you break the tribe's rules or laws, you are thrown out of the tribe.

Both the living and the dead are included in our tribe or "big family".

The dead live in the Kingdom of the Dead.
Sometimes they visit us. They come as a snake, a crocodile or a whirlwind. Sometimes they appear in dreams.

The dead have to be buried in the right way. We build small huts for them. We pray and make offerings to them. If you lose favour with the dead, they take revenge.

The dead live on in their children. When my younger brother was born we made offerings to the dead in our family. He was given the same name as my grandfather.

I have the same name as my great-grandfather.
My sisters are named after our grandmothers.
In this way, the dead remain among the living.

Our people are divided into groups according to age. Children, warriors, married people and the old make up the different age groups.

The men look after the cattle. The women must not touch them. They look after the home and the children.
They stay in the village while the young men go round the country with the cattle.

When girls have learned the skills of grown women, they can be married off.

The chief of the tribe is chosen by the people.
He is both king and priest. He is holy.
The chief makes sure that the tribe's customs are handed on. He sees to it that the laws of the tribe are obeyed.

When boys are between 12 and 16 years old they become murrani.

My brother Dokka is fifteen years old.
A few months ago he became a murrani. "Murrani" means warrior. A murrani is counted as a grown man.

For some time before he became a warrior, Dokka lived with the other boys of between 12 and 16. They learned everything a grown man should know.

They had to pass different tests to show that they were strong and brave.
When they had passed all the tests they were circumcised. Beforehand they were covered in white clay and all their hair was shaved off.

Dokka now lives with the other warriors in a camp.
The warriors can't marry before they're thirty.

There are spirits and powers in everything.

There are spirits and powers in wild animals, in stones, in mountains, in rivers and in trees. You have to keep in with the spirits otherwise they can be dangerous.

There are rules for how to behave towards the spirits. They are called the taboo rules. "Taboo" means holy or forbidden.

You must avoid things which are taboo. People, some food, some fruit and other things can be taboo.

I wear a fetish around my neck to protect me from evil forces. It is a small bag of plants which the chief gave me. Everyone has different fetishes. They can be the claw of an eagle, a piece of wood or an animal's tooth.

The witch doctor knows how to behave
towards dangerous forces.

The witch doctor can contact the spirits. He can also cure illness caused by the spirits. He knows the different secret medicines.

The witch doctor can also make it rain and he can make animals and people fertile.

The witch doctor can use magic to make the spirits do what he wants.

Magic is performed in many different ways. For example, you dance the rain dance and make splashing sounds if you want rain.

If you want to harm someone, you put pieces of glass in his footprints.
You make a doll that looks like someone you want to harm and stick pins in it.

Ngai is our chief god. He created the world.

Ngai decides everything that happens. He rules over the sky, the sun, the drought, the rain and the thunder.
We pray to Ngai when there has been a long drought.

We light a fire. We throw things in it and pray to Ngai to send us rain.

We have other gods that we pray to for help.
If our cattle do not produce young, we dance a fertility dance for the gods.

When my sister Banani was married we
had a big party.

Banani is 13 years old.
She married a murrani from
another tribe.
He had to give us lots of cows
as a "bride price" for her.
Now we have quite a lot of
cattle.

Banani has had to move from our
village. She now lives with her
husband's tribe. When he came
to fetch her we had a big party.
All weddings are performed in
the same way.

The purpose of these wedding
customs is to make sure that the
married couple have many
children. Otherwise the tribe
would die out.

The Indians in Peru

My name's Juanita and I live in Peru.

Peru is a mountainous country in South America.

I'm eight years old and I live with my father and mother and my seven brothers and sisters in Viru.
Viru is a village not far from Lima, the capital city.
Most people in Viru work on the land. We have a small piece of land which we cultivate.

As there are so many of us in the family, my father also has to work at the hacienda.
A very rich landowner lives there.

We are Indians. Our people, the Incas, were once a large and powerful people.
The Inca was our king; he was "the Son of the Sun". The Incas prayed to the sun.

Four hundred years ago the Spanish conquered the country. Christian missionaries came. Many of our people were converted to Christianity. Like most people in South America, we are Catholics. We have a church in Viru. Father Camillo is the priest.

The White God helps us if we pray to him. Sometimes that is not enough. Then we pray to the saints and to the old Indian gods, too.

It doesn't rain very much here. If there's a drought, nothing grows. Then we pray to the Maiden of Sorrows. We have a big fiesta in her honour every year on 12th December.

If we give her the right sort of celebration, it ususally rains. If it still doesn't rain we usually carry Saint Isidore's picture out into the fields. St. Isidore is the patron saint of farmers.

When the well-drillers came.

Last year strangers came to Viru to drill for water. There had been a long drought. They needed a lot of help. My father and the other men in the village did not want to help them. My father said that they did not want to disturb the water god.
If the water god became angry then we wouldn't have any water at all.

Once I went and watched the men drilling. They had nasty machines that roared and shrieked. It's much better to leave the water god in peace. Father Camillo thought so too and the men had to go back to town again.

Pedro is my eldest brother. He works in Lima. When he heard about the wells he laughed. Pedro thinks my father is superstitious. Offerings and prayers to gods and saints don't provide water, he said. Technology is better.

I think my father's right. When we've prayed to the water god or the Maiden of Sorrows they've sent rain.

There is a picture of the Black Madonna up in the mountains. Sometimes we make a pilgrimage there. The Black Madonna cures illness.

![A street scene high in the mountains with people walking down a dirt road between old buildings, mountains in the background]

High up in the mountains, in Cuzco.

Once I went to Cuzco with my family to visit relations. While I was there, there was a big fiesta in honour of the god Taitacha Temblous – an old Indian god who protects us from earthquakes.

Before Lent they have a carnival just as we do in Viru. We put on fancy dress and wear masks of the gods. We dance in the streets.

Many people from our village have moved to Lima.

Most of them are worse off than they were in Viru.
It's difficult to find work and their housing is bad.
Pedro has been lucky. He works at a factory.

In Lima the Indians are very poor, but they can pray to the Lord of Miracles. The Incas called him Pachacamac.

My father says that many who have moved into town are forgetting the old customs.
They no longer pray to the gods and saints. That's why they're having a hard time.
Others say it's because some people want to be rich.
They oppress the rest of us.